The Capricious Flight of Poems

MARY O. BREMIER

The Capricious Flight of Poems

ISBN   979-8-218-09944-2

Book design by Nan Barnes, StoriesToTellBooks.com

The Capricious Flight of Poems

Contents

Creation and Limitation

Transcendence

Nostalgia

Dedication

Paths and Portents

Guarding the Gates

There's a doorway to our minds
only we can enter
we know the terrain
divergent thoughts
see the mental clutter
feel the emptiness
or hear the music accompanying
inner peace

Inside there are many portals
firmly controlled and censored
as to who may enter or depart
what language may be spoken there
what truths may awaken sleeping hounds
lying by the gates

There is no way we can truthfully share
or comprehend how little we understand
at the crossroads of commerce
trading vibrations of inner worlds
for I can only half-speak
and you can barely hear.

I am my thoughts
the reflection of my thoughts
my words when spoken become half-truths
I cannot be my audience and stand away

to judge my inner lives
for I am the flow and the genesis of the flowing
nor can others ever know
how I dwell in meditation
or turbulent angst
for when I invite you in
the door is half-open
and you are somewhere else.

Knowing how far apart our worlds lie,
and the walls between us
I yearn for an evolution of language
a future when we can speak our truths
exchange thoughts entertained beyond speech
beyond duplicitous body language
I yearn to know and share
what brings us great joy
what unshaped stories inhabit our minds
that determine our destinies.

The Enduring Night

I welcome the enduring night
as I enter the darkest forest
lost, naked and unshod
I clothe myself in its textures
and robe myself with fear.

Entangled in the deep sea forest
commingling with primordial beings
in the secret passages and portals
I acknowledge myself,
and all beings inchoate
and fully-formed
ineffable
the unfathomable.

Entering the cave of memory
where terror and bliss collide,
sparking insight and humor,
the Sentinel,
my oldest ancestral spirit, waits
to hand me dreams and poems
shaped and stamped by the tortuous journey
through the enduring night.

The Crossroads

I'm resting at the crossroads
  before I go on
    to uncharted lands whose
      laws are unknown;
        there I linger
          and long for my home.

I'm breaking the tentacles
  that burrow in my brain
    and urge me to repeat
      the script I was taught.

I've walked in this desert
  with lost shadow-souls
    I could have known
      save for the myths
        that now are written in stone.

And the myths of belonging
  to a tribe or a place
    are forever gone.

The Bend

There is a bend on the path of life
that doubles back
giving an uncanny view of the past
of innocence transmuted into bitter wisdom
of dreams disappearing
like coins lost in unfair bargaining
passions cooling like molten metals

Hope
once emblazoning the way forward
like summer fireworks
is absent
leaving the path strewn with ashes
and ululations echo
drowning out laughter.

Shall we ever be wrapped
in the blissful blanket of self-acceptance
find a balm to ameliorate human suffering
or a salve that heals the pain
of feeling lost or unloved?

As reality crystallizes
at this bend

into a paradigm
of torment and travail
the dismally flawed nature
of humankind
looms large and grim
on all horizons

Forgiveness and love,
the balm
that restores and reshapes reality,
often comes late.

My Estranged Love

Drifting through streets and alleyways
I inhale your presence
this redolence impassions me
with anticipation of our lovemaking

My love, I yearn for your kisses on waking
as I salute the sun
you are my ode to joy
you distill my poetic inspiration
diffuse my depression
infuse me with confidence
I become volitant in my ascending rapture

O Coffee!
You make me feel alive at dawn
you keep me joyful by day
with an insatiate craving for our communions

Yet lately by night
you've sent me
to the mundane corners of my psyche—
it's a betrayal and a curse
I have grown weary of our connection
of my fitful wakefulness,
and midnight-TV-watching and worse.

Oh coffee,
now I am estranged from you
I am sleepy by day and dull at night
no stimulation, no elevation in sight
sadly, I need a dissolution of our union
I must claim grounds for divorce!

Primal Scream

I grope my way
through ever-lingering darkness
where the thorn-knitted thicket
smothers, chokes and tortures
and I become the scream
that echoes far
and finally fades in a void.

There's no path through this jungle
only the one I'm making
wading through murky waterways
toward sun-slanted rays
toward the mother-flesh warmth
of memory
where Need cries out

And I'm back.
I am here. It is now.
For now, my lamentation is over
but this racking trek cannot end
till the path is well-worn,
the journey familiar,
the pain predictable
and the knowledge secured.

It is this agonizing stretch
that heralds the respite—
the joy
I never would have known
save for the arduous trekking,
the dark groping
toward the light.

Perspectives

A female frog
  wept as her mate
    transmogrified
      into a prince.

Butterflies flutter
  their fragility
    over pale flowers.

High in a locust
  the raucous raven
    squawks stentorian sermons.

Silhouetted at dusk
  a bird warbles sweet memories
    of blue skies and light.

Children's boot prints
    spoil and sanctify
        virgin snow.

A gaudy macaw sits
    squawking rude remarks
        on God's lack of subtlety.

Gold, scarlet, purple
    sunset on churning waters
        God's on LSD again.

Outside looking in
    my life is a puppet show.
        who's tugging at my strings?

Points of Reference

How do you find your way in a land without boundaries
Where names of streets are written in foreign alphabets
Long and unpronounceable

In a woods where the trees are identical
No moss growing on north hillsides
In a place of solemn voices giving directions
Without points of reference

How do you find your way
When you first turn was wrong
And directions were given in the tongue of estrangement
And what will it help if you cry out and
Your wailing dirge is sung by choirs of lost voices

How will you find your way without star or compass
Your footprints stolen by the wind
And your map over-written with contradictory directions

And when you are "found"
still lost, bound and branded
Who can say where you are
have been, or are going?

Odyssey

Like poems
our lives are esoterically clear
fraught with luminous images
ringed by Rembrandt-darkness.

But only I can
write the poem of me
only I can write my Odyssey:

Tossed on a tormented sea
without knowing water,
I found my way home
without a guiding star.

Lost in a woods,
as a wolf child,
I sniffed out all that was human
and licked my wounds
as a wolf will.

After wending my way
through a labyrinth
of distrust and traps,
I limped home
now familiar with estrangement
and estranged from the familiar.

This is the poem
 of me—
this is my odyssey.

The Gaping Abyss of Time

I will live on the edge of Now
direful precipice of Time
I will not send my voice ahead
to echo in hollow places
nor ask prophets to announce
tomorrow's turn of events.

Here on the precipice
life is chancy
its story suspended

Yet somewhere new beginnings
are being composed
weaving and unraveling
and finely tuning multiple variables
into my narrative

From this edge
naively naked and open
to the drama of life
and the imminence of death

I will plunge
without line, chute or wing
into the gaping abyss of Time.

Fredrick

Somewhere from your book
My name was deleted
Or faded
Not as if you ran a line
Or crumpled the page as waste
But from a more common fate

My name disappeared
As time and distance
Set us on different paths

But in my mind
I find myself
Searching along your trail
Like a hound in pursuit
To know
Where our paths diverged or ended.

For fresh as ink, not yet dried,
Your name is etched in my mind
And your youthful face is framed.
I only need to know
How you grew old with time.

A Kiss Withheld

He didn't choose his nemesis
nor his defense against them
He never knew his demons
though flashes of their faces
haunted his night vision.

His battlefield from a fractured heart
enflamed wounds when touched
transformed him, into rage
the dagger's penetration, so deep
left wounds that could not heal.

He didn't choose his demons
nor his victims
they were thrust upon him
in battles he could not win.

And his own Sweet Angel,
that bright ray of focused thought,
who visited him so briefly,
withheld her healing kiss.

I Lift My Shades

Mornings
I lift my shades to the light
Evenings
I close them to the darkness

Days
Before me vanish into night
Too short

My race
Running toward each deadline
Hobbling over hurdles
Careening at sharp curves
Straining up hills
To the finish line
Deadline dead end

Looking backward over jilting time
Mornings I lift my shades
To the light
Evening against the darkness

The Race

I race with Time—
   always a lap behind.
      she teases me with what's undone
         leaving footprints in stone
            I run late
               failing to erase predestined
                  designs

Some say she's the warp
   interwoven with Space
      elusive
         ineffable
            yet meeting every deadline
               and winning every race

She teases me on like
   The Hare, the Tortoise --
      always a pace ahead
         I petition her
            to meditate awhile
               "The race doesn't matter,"
                  I say while watching the clock
                     damning the damage
                        of the ticking in my head
                           as she weaves and unravels
                              horrific truths
                                 of Age's revenge on Youth

as she weaves the warp and woof
of cause and effect
into the fabric
of an unrelenting cloth

Prayer cannot stop her
no gods will intervene
no going back
to homeostatic peace

I partner with denial
with redemption
with dreaming
I partner with Hope

Somber-faced Time
time of the sun
the Earth
clock of my universe,
I plead for mercy
for leniency
I started late so
must I conform
to *your* finish line—
my song has not been sung
and my dance has just begun.

Chasing Words

I spend my days
  chasing words
    as they play hide and seek
      tumbling jumbling
        sounds and syllables
          making their escape.

Once I was acquainted with the right word
  that knew its place
    in my thoughts
      now it stands on the cliff
        of my mind
          teasing before falling into an abyss.

Now it comes nearer
  chucking me under the chin
    here I am
      I entice it
        with honey-flavored feelings
          I loved you once
            can we love again?
              can we get personal?
                where did you come from?"
                  your first language
                    Greek
                      Latin
                        some Nordic cave-dwelling tongue?

I marvel
how far you've traveled
and how you've changed.

While spacing out and resting
from the chase
some beloved word whispers its name,
"Here I am
grab me if you can."
I catch it in midair
I'm in love again
but what was its intended context?
what brilliant thought
or grandiose idea
was it to express?

I hold this gem on my tongue
taste its essence
its definitions
let it ferment
inebriate my mind with love and delight.

Pendulum

Diurnal recurrence of cumulative sorrows
   weigh heavily in early morning hours
      they have no language
         no time nor place to attach themselves
         —sorrows churning up from dreams melded
mangled
            and fractured in a caldron of seething heartaches

Before sunrise chases the darkness
   seeking relief I consider baptismal water rituals
      wilderness wandering or prostrate prayer

But by now I should see
   how the cycles of the head and heart
      wind and rewind their reels of diurnal rhythms—
         light and shadows
            exhilaration and depression
            complacence and angst
               happiness and heartache

Shadows and Light

I Kept My Distance

I kept my distance from their deaths
I didn't want to know—
or feel it
its finality.

But the shadows of their being
come 'round the trees
and knock at my door
in dreams
to say "Hello,
it didn't happen,
you know."

I kept my distance
I didn't want to know
but Agony's persistence
told me "It is so."

Persephone at the Beach

I took my daughter to the beach
and watched the children gathering shells
to take home
in their sandy baskets

I see their braids in skipping gaits,
untied ribbons, wet and awry,
sandy legs and sunburnt foreheads
bent intensely
sculpting castles of sand and water

Gulls limned in silhouettes face the sea;
clouds caught aflame with Evening's torch
on the rim of churning waters.
Now their treasures lie in heaps
or taken home with sticks and stones
in sandy baskets.

Oh, the brilliance of summer days!
the sun--its brightness!
and oh, our cherished innocent daughters!
say a prayer for them now,
for the gap is deep
and swift on his coal black steed,
Darkness rides away with his quarry...
there will be no reunion with my daughter
and her shell-laden basket.

Judgement

I have had my own judgement day
and puny resurrection.
I, both judge and judged,
have seen my image
clearly in the cesspool of humanity
and will not; cannot
condemn another.

I've watched the spirits rise
over this swirling pit
in the morning mist
and have communed in their rites
seeking love and redemption
for a bewildered human race.

Bytes

Like bread not kneaded
half-baked
unleavened,
caged children
are set free
in the wilderness—

Wandering,
lackadaisically,
dumb to questions
to needed answers
children famished
on brain crumbs
machine-fed
to automated-mouths.

Haiku-ish

Leaves float and fall
Scribbling little poems
Gleaning the essence of life.

From a misty vale
Whippoorwills awaken a world
swaddled in solitude.

Fresh warm tears,
regurgitated pain,
wash my emotional slate
clean as morning rain.

Maids allured by songs of spring
create love nests
while crones sit looking askance...

He never spoke
except to say "excuse me"
he meant "for being"

The sun rose on promises
and set with them denied
Hope's Angel will fly in tomorrow

Spring is for callow youth;
sages awaken in fall
braiding flowers into old women's hair.

Children's noses fog window panes
flurries in the air
snow birds proclaim, "It's winter!"

At the wardrobe
what to wear
ah yesterday's clothing
still waiting on the chair.

The Cacophony of Madness

The cacophony of madness
    crescendos to a stormy finale
      shattering
        resounding
          lingering in empty balconies

Leaving arguments and arias
    and sacred song sheets
      to be lifted and mockingly fingered by the wind
      and the baton in the hands of buffoons

If only the mellifluent melodies could be gathered
    by the winds of mercy
      and the masters of music could
        bring back the sweet songs of sanity.

Monkey Monks

We sit in our cloistered
three-monkey cells
hearing, seeing, speaking
no more
of children
hungry, diseased, disabled
sold in markets
on cluttered streets
chained to the pain of powerlessness
captives of greed
the boot of the world
grinds upon them.

From our cloistered cells
the bells chime
"The eleventh hour
And all's well.
See no...
Hear no...
Speak no..."

Fat Cats Feast on Fossil Fuel

Fat Cats
   dine in dens of coal
      drink at spigots of oil
         excrete dollars and dirt
            in oceans
               that vomit the stench of carrion,
             of oil-drenched Death.

Fat Cats
   bow mawkishly before bloated banks
      and pay homage to dictators, power mongers
      and corruptible kings
         who trade in the currency of lives
         to appease insatiable appetites.

This malady spreads
   and as air chokes
      and oceans churn in discontent
         the Fat Cats belch their mantra
         "The Earth does not warm
         from our exhalation."

Speeding on addicted wheels
   along the tarred speedways across the land
      through plastic cities
         we pause to quench our thirst
         on the drug that poisons the world.

Fat Cats
   have no ears for the prognosis:
      that their pandemic appetite escalates
      the end of life on fragile earth
         to nature's ineffable creations
            and the destruction of civilizations

Noise

If the people knew
they'd storm the gates of nations
in outrage

So
it is of necessity
that the truth be whispered down
the air be filled
with idiot-making noise
that our senses
be blocked by commerce
transforming us into glazed-eyed
instruments
of the market place
while weary workers
trapped in submission
as permanent debtors
become virtual slaves

Oh if the people knew
the airwaves were theirs to tend
the awakened might cross moats
storm gates
crush walls of nation states
to repossess their rights

So
it is of necessity
that noise continues
LOUDER, and yet LOUDER
until the screeching decibels
deafens us all to truth.

Tools

Tools
extensions of the hands
indicator of one's superiority
to the lowly and less-tooled.

A tool
a wheel accelerating the work of the weary
rocks to build
to stone the unclean
to exact justice
at the market place
a stone, a guillotine, a rope
a bomb
tools.

Tools to invade
extract exploit exact
from the untooled
who fall into lowly ranks
jailed, enslaved

Tools—
extensions of the hands that rule

The Brooder

She sits like a brooding hen
she spreads her wings
over her clutch
of remembered pains
She nurtures them
keeps them warm
until they hatch
into fledglings
and become her reason
for living
and motive for dying.
then she drags them
among her life's weeds and thorns
the weeds of her life
giving them substance
and a life of their own.

Why Do I Fear

Why do I fear
  when from sunny meadows
    choirs of birds and insects
      announce pastoral bliss?

Why do I say
  an uneasy prayer
    for the young
      unschooled in the complexity of life
        when they zoom across my path
          wind-blown, sun-tanned and free?

There is some ghastly anticipation
  that clouds forming somewhere
    tempestuous shattering winds
      brewing on some unknown seas
        will fill these skies
          with the dark debris
            of old pains and new catastrophes

Why do I fear
  the cycles
    of white flags and surrender
      and the opiate music
        of life in repose?

Becalmed I become wary
    Sure that nothing blissfully quiet
      can persist in this body
        in this fitful world
          which undulates alternating waves
            of pleasure and pain
              and of war and peace.

Going West

His jeans hang low
belted below his bulbous belly
he swaggers in his cowboy boots
pronouncing his step
in exacting strides

His cigarette pasted on his lips
moves with his laconic words
blustering insecure manhood.

Having foresworn
all things sentimental
he knits his brows in disdain
for "Bleeding Hearts"
he calls them

Now perched high
headed west in his big Mack truck,
he blinks away his tears
like the wipers, the rain
as infant shoes
dangle from the rear-view mirror

Sun-Dappled Darkness

The dappled sunlight
reflecting the lace-curtain patterns on the floor
did not move her from her sadness.
After the cold winter months
she longed for such a sign.
but the sadness was deeper than she knew,
had accompanied her longer
than she had realized

Its origin was ancient and obscure
she stared at the patterned light
and reached her hand to catch it
changing its pattern and feeling its warmth.

Suddenly she understood the centuries
of sun worship as a searching
for a way out of the wintry darkness
conceived and incubated in the human heart.

Children-of-the-Book
(A prayer)

I

Oh, God of the Judeo-Christian Book
forgive us our transgressions
as we have not had an excellent model
of a Heavenly God.

Forgive us, your children,
if we are arrogant, perverse and cruel,
for you have shown us how to war
against one another, how to
to take prisoners and slay them,
but save the virgin daughters
as gifts to their great warriors
forgive our bloody wars
our torture, rape,
licentiousness and greed
which you have shown us well.
remember it is written in your book—
without apologies.

II

Lord-of-the-Book

you have shown us how to mete out imperfect justice

with absurd laws and harsh judgments.

you have taught men to dominate all that lives

upon the earth,

that women are perverse and unclean

having brought sin to a perfect innocent world,

that a price could be put on a woman's body,

and that wives could be bought and sold as cattle, barley

and even for foreskins of Philistines.

We remember how the warrior, Jephthah,

called upon you, Lord-of-the-Book,

promising a sacrificial offering

of whomever from his door came first.

he must have known it'd be one of his own

so eager for his return.

Jephthah's daughter resplendent with joy

came first, greeting him tenderly.

There was regret.

There was sorrow.

There were cries for mercy,

but no turning back.

no recanting.

youths' must be sacrificed—

must appease the God-of-War.

III
And what lesson must we learn
from the daughters of Shiloh,
who came to dance,
not knowing men were hiding in the vineyards
to capture them.

And of Lot, who offered his daughters to rapists
to protect his guest from ill-treatment
as a show of hospitality.
and what of the concubine
raped unto death,
body dismembered,
whose body parts were sent to the twelve tribes of Israel?
what morals are we to learn?

David
captured Bathsheba to be a bride
(as if he needed one more wife)
and arranged the death of her husband.
Lord-of-the-Book,
was it right
to kill a man and take his wife?

You bewail, "Who can find a virtuous woman?
for a virtuous woman must adorn herself
with modest apparel
and be shamefaced, silent and sober—
for woman wrapped in gold is a whore."

You condemn the daughters of Zion saying,
"They are haughty walking with out-stretched necks
and wonton eyes
walking and mincing as they go
making a tinkling with their feet."
confess, Lord-of-the-Book,
were you not tempted by their beauty—
by their confident sexuality?
must you deny your proclivity
by shaming the daughters of Zion—
and discovering their secret parts?

And Aholiboh
was desired and desiring of gorgeous men,
and God-of-the-Book,
upon your orders, the men descended upon her
to take her nose, her ears
and leave her naked
to pluck off her own breasts.
Why?

And God-of-the-Book,
why did you hate Nineveh
you say because of its well-favored harlots
mistresses of witchcrafts

You condemn witches
who are said to arouse men and cause impotence
and change men into beasts.

You denounce them all,
with a merciless law:
"Thou shalt not suffer a witch to live."

And so we, the Children-of-the Book,
burned thousands at the stake,
believing that women had such powers,
and feeling righteous as we lit the pyres.

IV
You tested Job's patience and his love
with torture
and Abraham, too, demanding sacrifice
of his beloved first son
to be slaughtered on your altar.
still, you, trickster that you are,
just checking his loyalty, his willingness
to give his best to you,
had a lamb ready,
for there had to be blood.

There had to be blood,
even of your own son.
we see him still
humble messenger of peace and love
hanging on the cross,
writhing in pain,
crying piteously.
Have you forsaken me?

Ultimately, mythically,
you drew him to yourself unharmed
deus ex machina
to your kingdom in the sky.

Now, tortuous images
of him hanging on crosses
in temples of peace
across the lands
recalling the days of human sacrifice.
can there be no peace
without spilled blood—
without human sacrifice?
must we drink wine turned into blood?

V

Lord-of-the-Book,
you command us to worship you
but how can we
steeped in cruelty as you are?
redeem yourself
shed your pagan cloak
come to us naked
before calling us to worship.

Forgive us, your children,
if we are vindictive, arrogant and cruel.
forgive our bloody wars
our torture, rape,

our licentiousness and greed
for you have taught us well.
remember, it is written there—
without apologies.
God-of-the-Book,
forgive us
lost and bewildered as we are
wandering among the pantheons
of the earth
in search of a perfect paradigm
of a Heavenly God.
inadvertently, we come home to you.
sadly, we are still your children,
Children-of-the-Book.

VI

The children of myths, legends and prophies
harboring among the groveling guilt-ridden
have searched among the pantheons of civilization
for a perfect paradigm of a heavenly God,
but have created Gods that mirror
the most primitive and punitive elements of their own
minds.

I say, it is now time to break away-
to come home to the self
while honoring the Gods, myths and ancient texts
as poetic products of creative minds of the past.

Let us now recognize ourselves
as the mysterious multi-faceted creatures
we have evolved into being,
and find our inspiration and salvation
rooted in love, logic, and truth.

Wounded Hawk

A wounded hawk wandering through
the undergrowth of the desert
shudders with fear.
remembering
when she soared,
she clings to her images of expansive skies
woodlands and mountains.

Cramped in a minuscule world,
peering out for possible prey,
crouching and cowering from predators,
her heart has grown small and weak,
cold and isolated
she searches quietly for comforting coves
to assuage her stark existence.

You wounded ones
huddling in the undergrowth
licking your wounds with hope
remembering the things of beauty
long sucked into the shadows of sorrow
I know you
the scars that cover your hearts
your longing to ride on the winds
to open your windows
to the world of broad expanses.

I say, go to the mountains and valleys
to the wilderness where wolves howl;
cry out your pain
till your ululations echo back as laughter
till you know the full spectrum of emotions,
the hallmark of being human.

Leningrad and Light

When God said
let there be light
there was scintillating shimmering light
magnifying itself on the water
and creating, evolving and sustaining life.

Light, was fractionated by water
into color and art,
creating love and beauty.
it became the metaphor
for brilliance of mind
the luminance of spirit
and another name for god.

In the absence of light
there was death
so we built bonfires on hilltops
to raise the disappearing sun.
we brought evergreen branches inside
to sustain and sanctify life
and spilled our own cherished blood on alters
so that the sun might not wane
our world into darkness and death.

Peter the Great,
wandering the streets of Venice
came to know the healing of light and water

and built the Venice-of-the-North
where beast preyed through the long dark days
on peasant builders
building a city of light.

So, when the June sun rose to the edge of the world
like a magical bonfire
and those that were drowsed and depressed
from the long dark days
awoke and walked in continuous light and peace
along the canals and rivers
that mirrored the radiant sun,
they knew the healing of light and water.

Jesus, teacher of love and righteousness,
accepting the metaphor of light and water
was baptized in the glimmering light of the Jordan
as a ritual for cleansing and affirming life

The dazzling illuminating light,
became a metaphor for truth
so, the obscure and uncertain
was made clear and concrete
and all that was to fear
was the absence of light.

Senility or Dyslexia

All traffic stops
for road blocks
strategically placed inside the passages
where Nouns (most suspect) are held hostage
and searched for meaning and form.

Those captured were your friends
you knew them well
and understood nuanced meanings
and feelings that accompany them.

Once you sang them on the free ways
and didn't argue at the gateposts
where searchers feel in every pocket
going up and down the alphabet
to see where they're hiding
to sabotage your way.

Then one day
you can't spell February
or your neighbor's name
and other words elude you.

February

you know it starts with F-E-B
but the rest is lost
and you are lost
as you were lost in corridors of another hemisphere
and you still don't know which way to turn
to the central place where you began.
the woods you loved is a maze you fear
for you have turned off often
and are lost in many ways.

Do you understand
 how confusion holds you hostage
how when February's spelling is a blank
or there's a lost word hindering your way
you wonder
if it's an ancient cataclysmic assault
or Senility playing his inane game
at tearing down the infrastructure of the brain.

Remember ah (REMEMBER?)
how you celebrate
when a hostage is released
like right now
(here comes February
lumbering under its two "R's"
too late.)

But then there's March and April
with only one "R' to tangle with your brain
with the broken pathways
and knotted threads that dangle to confuse.
still you wish for a simpler way
as you whiff the scent of flowers
and think of May.

Do you understand
how wonderful it is to celebrate
released hostages
and dance them on your tongue
like a fine wine?

Creation and Limitation

You, in the Mirror
(Self-Analysis at 93)

I put my glasses on
I examine my makeup
my face comes into focus
every line clearly and largely defined
this wasn't supposed to happen to me!
me, whose body houses an adolescent,
vibrantly reactive two-year-old,
a megalomaniac
whose work to save the world
has barely begun.

And I've aged.
like an onion
its exterior dried and yellow
as an old sage,
but inside, the layers are separate and individual—
some rather callow.
My mouth clinches together into a thinner straighter
line—
holding something in part of me wants to blurt out.
my joints like an unattended hinge
groan and complain.

You in the mirror
I don't want to be so hard on you.
Even before you appeared before me in this old
woman's garb
your internalized mother
was harshly judgmental.
Such judgment extends and colors
my more global pronouncements
so I appeal to the Goddesses—
my inner best layers-
somewhere within
to loosen my mouth and soften my judgment
giving more compassion toward me and others
helping me to rear the two-year-old dissident within,
nurture the romantic,
and give the megalomaniac a truer view of the world,
so that this old onion can spring roots,
send forth greenery in its own springtime,
and celebrate the coming of age
in its own season.

A Moment on Stage

Interrogator puts spotlight
  on Ego
    standing on stage
      blinking
        proclaiming, defending
          creating an image

I am, I am not
  narrowly defined
    for sale
      at this price
        on this market
          nor an object
            propelled like a puppet
              by a ventriloquial voice
                from behind the curtain.

Critic stands ajar
  An out-of-body-experience
    judging from accumulated minds
      from standards
        of other worlds…

Till in quandary by query
  superego steps on stage
    creating a unifying bliss
      of ego-less-ness

A moment
        out-of-culture
Now light
   pierces down
      with an inexpressible knowledge
       of me, I, the web of life
         all segments
            of the priceless
               unifying whole of existence.

Pastel Picture

I stand
before my canvas
framed in black
the center
vermillion
waiting to burst
like northern lights
across my universe

This confined passion
dialectic of my inertia
trapped by fear
cool whites
and icy blue
fear of color
of the covert scarlet center
the dormant verve.

In lame defiance
of this inertia
I paint in pastel passions
and peaceful whites
fogging over grim gray grief,
I frame
before my world
A painted canvas
Its center still waiting
Waiting

Shards Of Peace

While finding my way
  through the shambles of my mind
  defining my direction
    I sift through the shards
      for repetition in design.
        thoughts and feelings
          are caught on treadmills
          or frozen in time,
            as symbols masking meaning
            unveil themselves
            in the light

Piece by piece
  the shards connect
    fit into place
      making the vessel whole,
        and the seams, the scars,
          reveal new designs
          defining my life
            shaping my new direction

Procrastination

How do I avoid thee
let me count the ways
I clean, I walk
and wash the walls
and even the oven
Things I would never do if my writing
were not lying
talking to me
scolding me from there
scattered on my table
where for two weeks
you have castigated me
"Sluggard, impotent imbecile,
Why did you start me
if you didn't intend to finish?"

How do I avoid thee
let me count the ways
a must-see movie
Amy Goodman on the radio
recounts a new scandal
so how, you-lying-on-my-table,
did you attain such precedence
in a world that could explode
any minute now
because of some political machinations?

How do I avoid thee
in countless ways
my headaches, it's time to eat
and I am tired and in need of sleep
you who-on-the-table-lying
make me weep
yet you are my life.
even you
who have given me a voice
are silencing me
by the burden you impose.

That voice lying on the table
the one that was once silenced
the one that stuttered to be free
from a fettering family
from rigid boundaries rationalized
as religious righteousness.

I say to you-on-the-table waiting
where the last chapters
of my voice lies
wanting to be finished—

I will not be silenced
by sleep, by tears, by nervous agitation
I will sit me down and write
When?!
Now?

Wind at my Back

When
  I flew against the wind
  (or) swam upstream

    when
      I chose the thorny paths
      of toil and sacrifice
        I applauded myself
          for sheer survival.

But when
  I turned away
    the wind to my back
      (or) leaving my paddle behind,
      sailing swiftly downstream

        movement was rapture
        struggle unknown;
          creativity and joy
          sent me on
              winged with a full-throated song.

The Mermaid of Sand

Wandering along the beach
  among sandy heaps
    I found a monumental beauty—
      a mermaid sculpted of sand

Voluptuous mounded breasts
  medusa hair
    Mona Lisa smile

Why?
  who took the time
    for whom
      and how far
        have I come
          in my survival-driven world
            from the world of play

That I marvel
  at this colossal ephemeral mermaid
    swimming her way
      out to sea.

A Delicate Flower

A delicate flower
brushed its softness against me
seducing me to stay longer
to meditate its meaning.
I wanted to envelop its beauty
to fuse with its freshness.

Was ever a flower
taken directly into heart
without the desire to hold it
describe or own it—
to put it in a vase?

And so our love
is put into a vase;
but it will not be encased,
for love is a delicate flower
determines its own season
and roots where it will
eluding words or reasons.

Doilies

She never chose motherhood
it was thrust upon her
a harness of duty
a cross to bear

She wished for warmth
from a cold dark place
where she crocheted doilies
and dreamed of velvet parlors

She crocheted silence
around my desperation
for a love that would not give
from where it was imprisoned
entangled in knotted patterns.

Poetry?

Is a poem a poem
in a woods read aloud
echoed in the branches of trees
but unheard by a crowd?

Are some eloquent lines
in a file unpublished
unread in a poets' forum
a poem??

Can a poem ruminated in the mind
warrant recognition
for its thought and inspiration
if it isn't transposed to paper by pen?

If I converse in iambs
without pentameter or rhymes
in insightful quotable lines
then is it poetry?

We're all anthologists
barking poems—good and bad
so when and how
might a muse ignite
the right synaptic site
and spark mere speech
into elegant sapient lines?

Is this a poem?

Moments of Contrariness

When told I *must* walk a straight line
The sideways and winding paths beckon.
When told I *must* tell the truth
great imagination
For possible prevarications
Whirl to mind.

When told I *must* be good
The dark recesses of my mind
Loom to consciousness
Conjuring up evils previously unthinkable.

When told I *must* be neat
I am drawn to disorder.
When told I *must* think
My mind trips away
With thoughts chasing thoughts
About *not* thinking.

When told I must write
Words wriggle away,
And thoughts so simple to say
Complex themselves
Into incomprehensible puzzles.

Inventing a Myth

Pegahorn,
Born under the sign of Capricorn,
Was the beautiful daughter
Of a unicorn
Who was married to Pegasus
He had no horn
But better still, had wings.
He soared
Was never bored
Was a delightful father to Pegacorn.

Pegacorn
Was born
With a small blunt horn
And like her father she had wings
Shorter than his
But still, her long mane streaming behind,
Propelled her wings
So she could fly
Higher in the sky
With Pegasus

Mother Unicorn
Watched their joyful flights
Days and nights

Until the Goddess of Wings
And other things
Invented wings of gold
And attached them to Mother Unicorn

Now the three fly
Higher than ever
Over moon, clouds and trees
Enjoying the sights of green planet Earth
Lifted ever upward by balmy summer breezes.

Capricious Flight of Poems

Poems fly down from a lofty plane
  where elfin minds concoct word-puzzles
    into verses.
      they come to me
       unannounced
         as if a royal guest landed
           in my kitchens over cooking
            disturbing recipes—
              too busy to write them down

Come midst conversations—
  muddling contrapuntal thought
  and disappearing lines

Come on the freeways
  a traffic snarl
    demanding concentrating
      erases every word

At night and early morning hours—
  too cold to push the covers back
  and not a pen in sight.

Poems fly through the air
  and evanesce
    like kaleidoscopic dreams
      losing their color
        midway in telling.

Poems don't want to be writ
    but a skillful wit
        will fetch them back
            will noose them in midair
                tame them
                    frame them
                        arrange them as flowers in a vase—
                    making art of life.

My dear capricious inconstant Muse,
    come down from your lofty space
        arrange my thoughts into fitting lines
            bring magic to my words
                come whenever
                    wherever
                        keep writing love songs to my mind.

Poems, out there wherever you are,
    please keep coming my way
        I'll hang a snare toward the wind
            strain and train my memory
                to secure your soft sweet landings—
                and gentle joyful births.

A Wingless Muse

Once a muse visited me
  not an elegant muse
  a wingless disheveled muse
  and wrote a poem for me
  that lifted me on wings
  to soar
  above a flat terrain
Till
I found it was a silly poem

Yet
it'd set me soaring for a while

Now
I welcome any muse
I open up my door
and fearing to implore
I gently invite her in.

The American Dream

The American dream, a cliché,
a belief system, a hopeful wish,
or is it a meaningless mantra?

Is it a simple birthright
to have time to play
sing with the singers
dance with the dancers
to revel in the poets' lines
to inherit the wealth of the land?

Is it a dream of freedom from want
a ladder propelling one upward
and onward to privileges
and the benefits
of the resources in other lands
where people wake with their dreams
stolen by American Dreamers?

Who dares dream that dream
and who decides
what dreams we may have?
is this dream American
or a dream without borders,
usurped and stolen
by the Robbers-of-Dreams?

Restraints

Restrained love
freezing in the veins
damming up tears
squeezing and flattening out life.

Restraints
ropes and chains
bars and barbed wire
vaults and walls
dank dark cells
boundaries and turfs
ownership and dispossession—
diminishing us all.

Tightened lips
stuttering tongues
silenced speech
censored thought
coil the mind
into a fetal state
of waiting—
frozen by time
and emerging
stillborn.

Wolf Children

Wolf children of the world
feeding on wild milk
and withered grasses in high deserts
hiding in unchartered hinterlands

Never nourished
wrapped in rags
you wander swollen-bellied
along mountain ranges and dessert dunes
as your bark and howl is diminished
to silent wails

Roaming in packs
a blight
to those who dictate and bend boundaries,
you're beaten back farther afield
as you nurse on the befouled teats of the earth.

Cradle Board

Jacob was a Puritan
    sat straight
    stood tall
        knew what should be
        or shouldn't have been
        and voiced disapproval
        of the perversions
            and sins of others.

If once he had danced
    laughed aloud,
        admitted a fault,
            or bent from his Puritan stance
            the pale aura of his childhood
            might have deepened
                into golden drops of delight
                and the child within freed
                from the restraints
                    of his cradle board.

Unglazed

God! Are we unfinished!
  a lump of unsculpted clay
    not ready to hold water
      borrowed ornamentation
      unbaked
        unglazed.

And yet
  we would be formed and reformed
    coiled
      and glazed with incandescent truth
        set in the oven of celestial fire
          made solid
            that we might hold this gift of life
              in a vessel made sacred
                by the rites of the Gods
                  of broken shards
                    and unfinished pottery.

If We Could Speak our Minds

There is a doorway only I can enter
that leads to where I alone can be.
I know the terrain I've constructed there—
rivers of peaceful thought
and music that accompanies it
divergent entangled pathways,
cluttered ornamentation,
the emptiness and dark silence,
turbulence and paralysis,
hurdles and ghoulish dead-end traps.

There is no speech to tell you—
For we cannot comprehend
How little we understand
At the crossroads of commerce
Trading vibrations of inner worlds
For I can only half-speak
And you can barely hear.

I am the thought and the reflection of my thought,
for words no sooner spoken than become half-truth
Nor can I as audience stand away
to judge my inner life,
for I am the flow and the genesis of the flowing
nor can you ever know
how I dwell there in serene meditation
or turbulent angst

For when I leave that place
I will don my robe for rituals
To greet a world of surface meanderings
Knowing how far apart these worlds lie
I will look into your eyes
As I yearn for an evolution of language
When we can speak our truths,
Joys and pains at a depth that
Now has no words

War of Words

They took my words
leaving me hollow
with nothing left to say
they forced their thoughts
into my brain,
a warring place—
invaders of an empty space,

Until at last
I marched against the foes
of thought
their reasoning
and found a voice
my Own.

Transcendence

Did Her Spirit Linger

When my mother died
did she break those tentacles of torture
drawn taut and tangled
within her flesh
and as she became flaccid and numb
did Death steal away
with its bag of bones
her smoldering pain?

And did her spirit rise
immortalized as the phoenix
soaring for sunlight
to rest among the green leaves
that speak of life and renewal of itself?

Or did her spirit linger
to dwell on my visage
to direct the drumbeat of my heart
and shadow my way along her path
to our ancestral home?

The Sting

You came into bed with me last night
laughing; stealing my warmth
for your little feet and legs were cold
against my body
I held you tight cuddling
you in my arms
we laughed together

When I realized you were wearing the dress
you wore when last I saw you,
you crumpled in my arms—broken
and I awoke
knowing finality and separation—
the sting of heartbreak
Again
Again

Introspection
Conversational Meandering on the Meaning of Life
(to be read by two voices)

Would you like to say something profound
As you breathe your last breath—
Words winnowing the essence of your being here?

What would it mean?
Are my words spoken near death
More significant than those of childhood
Or midlife when flattened out
of hopes and ambitions?

What do you want for an epitaph?

What do I want them to think?
Will it matter?

What happens now—will it finally accumulate
    And form a crystalline distillate of you?

Maybe I'm multiple, like the moods
And moments of my existence—
* Maybe it's all an amorphous meaningless mass*

Or like a drama--
A slow crescendo into a cloud-bursting climax
Followed by a neatly folded denouement.

More like an endless road
With varying scenery along the way,
Inducing sundry and random thoughts.

And schemes to get home
Around the next curve.
Yearning for the next turning
Until it all abruptly stops.

Do you think there are peak experiences?

More like punch lines for me
And some proverbial bits of wisdom
Garnered here and there.

But there's an intense desire for drama—
Meaning and action.
A willful wandering away—
Being lost…

Yes, and a need for the struggle homeward—
To be with oneself at last.

Why

Why have I not
understood fully
life's a gift

Why this sentence
to work and survive
a trial
an end goal
report card
judgment day

Day and night
little twilight
for reflection
to savor the moment
to feel the sensuality of being

To internalize
the still point
of self-definition
chills in the spine
eyes opening wide
a total response
to love music art color
being vibrantly alive.

Joy

Joy came to my door
  uninvited
    without a message
      entering
        she anointed me
          with her grace
            and sent me soaring
              to her music

Then she gathered her grace
  unto herself
    leaving me
      to my mundane existence
        confounded by her mystery.

Free Fall

I have gazed on open seas
barricaded by walls
tethered to a lifetime
of timid ambitions
Philosophies grounded in ancient cultures
not relevant to a life that yearns
to break through whatis
into the open-ended whatmaybe.

There is in me a yearning
to thrust into infinite space
or lands beyond my recognition
a calling to learn
what else there is
besides my bread, my joys and fears

I have dreams
to let go of my tight holding on
and thrust myself into midair
of breaking the umbilical
of the world that has nurtured me
I have dreams of abandoning
this ancient human cave.

I have gazed on open seas
and yearned to explore its depths
and fluid highways,

but how to let go
of this holding on?

It's the fear of separation
this yearning for home
for tradition
the familiar

This fear keeps me bound
save in dreams
dreams of a free fall
into infinite space
where destinations are unknown
paradigms shattered
knowledge transformed
by an ineffable realization
of what is possible in me
and all humankind.

On Listening to Lakme's Flower Duet

Dare I be so exhilarated,
so uplifted by the sound
of Celestial songs
that transform/transcend?
Dare I venture
on to the other side
to passion so deep
so loving
so open to giving?

Dare I
leave reality stranded
and glide through this chamber
of Euphoria,
enraptured by the gods,
and drunk on the nectar of Love?

Dare I
enter this hallowed temple
this private paradise
replete with self-love
that expands and extends
in an embrace
of all humanity?

Yes
I dare—for this moment
I'll leave reality stranded
and ascend on wings of love.

Embrace

Give me a potpourri of life:
some of the wisdom of a savant
the rhythm and magic of an exotic dancer
love expressed in a Spanish song

Let me meditate in the moonlight
while gazing at stars
as if from Everest's heights

Give me arms long enough
to embrace all of humankind:
our ignorance, darkness and innocent errors
our ingenuity, patient labor and insightful art
our wonder and discoveries.

May my arms be so long!
And may humanity stretch them farther!

Untethered

I flew my kites high
with great control
when the winds soared them wild
my calm
brought them down.

Once in a blizzard
my kite grew turbulent
tearing them from my grasp
they flew like drunken birds
in wild ecstasy
fluttering beyond
my sight.

When I freed my entangled strings
one stormy day
the wind took them
beyond my horizons.

well aware
that someone might catch them
I breathed
a prayer
for their escape.

And that you,
my soul mate of flight,
might soar
without restraint

and I,
understanding the heights
to which you have disappeared
thrill to the joy
of freedom's song
for I, too,
am un-tethered.

A Pillow is not Enough

A pillow is not enough
to embrace in the night
a comforter does not comfort
against the chill
a prayer is not enough
to ward off the fear
of life spiraling
toward death.

Philosophical meanderings
do not bring serenity
no book explains
how to block dark memories
or assuage the pain
of loss

Yet

I must remember
tsunamis that batter the land
recede
new life springs from debris
and new dreams are born

I must remember
how Dawn spreads her golden fingers
into the windows of my world
banishing darkness
inviting light within.

Outside the Box

Now I walk parallel to
  perpendicular with
    at right angles
      right about face
        controlled
          punctuated and stopped
            by metered lights,

But in dreams I
  move diagonally,
    fly vertically,
      jump fences,
        tease bulldogs,
          romp through inverted arches,
            dwell in hyperbolic houses,
              skip on my hands
                viewing flowerbeds
                  planted zigzag among signs
                    "Walk through me – please!
                    Trespass by and beyond
                      the stale geometry of rigid minds
                        of Dollar-Per-Square-Foot
                          with no variances allowed!"

Soaring on Love

Last night I dreamed we were together again
Our bodies closely wed
Our minds attuned like an orchestra
And we soared on the same pair of wings

I dreamed last night we were together again
We sang in harmony
Your voice, the bow that stroked my heart strings
And we soared on the same pair of wings

I dreamed last night we were together once more
And our stormy days were gone
The sun shone like the smile on your face
As we soared on the same pair of wings

This morning I woke to find you are gone
And seeing it was only a dream
The echo of your voice broke my heart's strings
While I plummeted on melted waxen wings

Last night I dreamed we were together again
Our bodies closely wed
Our minds were attuned as an orchestra
As we soared on the same pair of wings
We soared
And soared
On the same
The same
Pair of wings

Stars

We are the millions
memories,

ready to break through
shaping images so beautiful
and strange
kaleidoscoping our fractured dreams,
making meaning
instantly understood
and forgotten.

We are the millions
memories,

we are everything
and everyone
we are stardust
born in terror and in bliss
formed in the flicker
of evening fires
mirrored in animals' eyes,

We are the millions
memories,

memories
dormant and alive,
crystalized into the historicity
of humankind

I Saw That Tree

Suffice it to say
  I saw that eucalyptus

Its silver leaves in the sun
  among olive and forest green
    and mottled trunk
      of rose and earthen orange
        curling textured browns
        sacred white
          and shameless satin nakedness.

I saw it with every cell of my seeing
  and in that seeing
    have known and trusted myself
      with a willingness to see, again,
        even if that means
          letting all else go by.

Nomad

Nomad of the heart
pitches her tent
in high arid places
where sand and wind storms
pierce her flesh.

She views the oases below
where torrential rivers
nourish flowering meadows
and gentle breezes
kiss the lands with life and fortune
and resolutely turns away

Nomads move to higher grounds
of massive lifeless dunes
To look toward violent sunsets
while meditating
the virtues
of solitude.

Forgiveness

"Forgive." What does it mean?
  Can the Jews forgive the Nazis?
    the Armenians, the Turks
      the Bosnians, the Serbs
        or you and I, adversary?

Are the wounds too deep
  the hurt inaccessible
    ancient or convoluted?

Are the pains of yesteryears
  encoded in our cells?

Forgiveness is not to forget
  to repress
    scar over festering wounds
      to smother flames of anger
        smudging the heart in anger's ashes.

For pain will ascend, it will erupt!
  suppressed, it will speak
    eloquently without knowledge,
      fomenting vengeful actions.

Can the pain of admitting guilt
  be worse than perpetuating conflict
    does it not require more remorse,
      more humility and more humanity?

Can we sing songs or hold hands
    or meditate it away?
        can we trick our hearts with false love?

Forgiveness requires clear insights
    into our own defenses—
        the willingness to communicate
            and rebuild connections!

To forgive we must grieve
                over our trespasses or having been wronged
                    for grieving ameliorates our pain
                        so we may feel at our heart's deepest level
                        the pain of our adversary.

A Cinderella Prayer

There Truth stands
staring me in the face
why do I detour
when she clearly maps my way?

Why muffle the voice
commanding me
to drop this garb
let go of the lost slipper
to stand naked
among the rats and cinders
while noting the desolation—
the loss of delusory dreams?

Truth, send me on
map my way,
free me
of false dreams and diverging paths
brighten

        enlighten my way.

Sunrise

I will not let the noise of this world
distract me from Wonder
at the morning sun
that awakens sleepy clouds,
drapes the earth in painterly colors,
and sustains all that is,
and me, with a limited understanding
that lets me wonder.

I will not let the things undone
nudge at my elbows
and dispel my wonder
nor will I let the spoils of yesterday
heap around my door and shut out Wonder
of me and all that is.

I will not let him who says
"this is the way it is"
lead me on a singular path
that strides blindly past Wonder
I will not let him.

I will invite diversity to my table,
feast on ambiguities and infinite possibilities
and besot myself from the cup of Humor.

I will dance and flirt with Wonder
with the delight of a laughing child
chasing pigeons in a park.

Nostalgia

Memories

(Christmas 1932, age 7, from a window facing North)

Looking up;
  I'm going up
    Dark flakes
      Floating down
        Landing white
       On white.

Elbows on the sill
  I look
    Toward the wooded North hill.

As flaming cardinals land
  Like fire,
    Black birds
      Squabble conferring
     Where to go.

They say
  The window faces north
    And there's a pole.
     On the wooded hillside
      "Must be Santa's home."
     I surmise.

So, I strain my eyes
  To see if he's there
    And see movements of brown
     That could be Santa's reindeer.

And I look and I long
  And I look for red
    And a belly ballooning
      Like a loaf of bread.

Breathing mist on the pane
  I continue to stare
    As I pray to the Red Man
      For a soft teddy bear.

I Remember Christmas

I remember Christmas
    Santa Claus and baby Jesus
        wishes and mysteries
            the waiting and the longing
                while watching by windows
                    cardinals landing on snow

I remember foreign fruit
    juicy, round
        and orange, Brazil nuts,
            horehound candy
                and my baby doll
                    wearing green pajamas

Now the mystery is gone
    first the jolly old man
        then the gift-bearing kings
            went back to their kingdoms
                and their dogmas
                    and the miracles that swaddled
                        Baby Jesus vanished with disbelief.

But there's a little bit of Christmas
    in me yet.
        I'll sing Handel's Messiah
            with many voices rejoicing
                and when the echoes of the hallelujahs
                    in the great hall have died

there will be a silence,
   a longing and a prayer
     for some soon coming
    of a prince
       robed in a voice of silver
      guiding us
        to a realm of peace

There's a little bit of Christmas
  in me yet
   I'll wear a red dress
    hang mistletoe and tinsel
     sing carols in my kitchen
      remember days long gone,
       my siblings who've died
        and the wishes and the mysteries
        that brightened our days
         like cardinals landing on snow.

Bay Area California Poets of Earlier Times

Drunken sad California poets
lovers of Tamalpais
read poems to each other
in dark places
hidden from the machinery of the world.
Young poets sought
enlightenment
in the far corners of their brains
LSD and mescaline took them there
where they wrote multilayered lines
in holy languages of gurus
chanting mantras in haunted caves.

Currents crashed across
the hemispheres of their brains
forging new pathways
like tornadoes crossing
the forest laying level
the trees
constructing new routes to unknown lands.
Their fractured lines
reflect remotely where
they had been/experienced
they invite others to join them—
to see the kaleidoscopic light.

Sad California poets left dusty pages
in the archives of time
Now who will resist the currents of time
the torrents of trends
the whirlwinds of gossip
or bend their minds
to meditate upon their sanctified lines?

Dorothy

Dorothy, a minimalist at art and writing
and in other ways, too
Oh how we loved the way you dramatized
those brief lines
of Dorothinian wit.

I came to know you better
after you left the class
declining in speech and mobility
at Nordstrom over lunches
where you were most articulate
expressing your secret loves
always surprising me
when after long silences of arrested speech
with clearly-articulated gems
of mischievous wit.

Your humor was there still
as more words were lost
and the end of sentences failed to materialize
You laughed when I searched for words
a way of saying, "You, too."
We had that in common, that searching for words lost.

When your hands and eyes failed you
you smiled after cutting at your food without success
And when you opened your mouth wide
for the non-existent food on your fork
Yet you refused my offer to help.
stubbornly independent until the last, you were.

Yet a few days before you lost it all
you handed me your lipstick
And I painted your mouth a vibrant red
And smiling
you blotted your broad smile on my cheek.
Was that your minimalistic way of saying Goodbye?

Katharine

I remember Katharine
older than her years
in her braided crown
and Mama combing and tying up
that silken hair
to make it seem shorter
and her to look like the child she was.

I remember the voile dress
with roses
she made for me
with an under slip with lace

I remember the plaid dress
the collar she invented
the designs she sewed on it
and the sash that tied behind.

I remember
the Easter Sunday school program
she organized
she was poised and sure of herself
as I stood in patent leather shoes
trembling at the knees
forgetting my lines.

I remember Katharine
coming home stylish and smiling
after a session in college;
how she engaged our parents
with her stories!

I don't remember
us playing games
or talking of romantic love
or confiding, fighting,
or making up;
I wish we had;
I wished we could have
we were too serious,
secretive and disciplined for that!

I remember Katharine
a child, having to be strong,
but I also remember her
growing up gentle and beautiful
filled with radiant hope.

Winter Clothes

I don't put winter clothes away
anymore
summer comes
sooner than before
she barely winks her bright eyes
and winter's here once more.

Remember when days were dreamy-long
and seasons distinctly marked and languid
now they run
shamelessly into one another
bumping off years like days.

Brilliant-Summer-Sun
goddess of fecundity
stay longer
while I inhale the balmy air
disrobe and invite
your light into myself.

Stay
stay till my blood runs warm again
with memories sensuous and sweet
till I've enough of light and heat
before winter chills the flesh.

I don't put winter clothes away anymore
the chill is coming soon.

Portrait of B.J.B.

She never wanted
more from life
than health
hot tea in a breakfast nook
wine on the lake with friends

But as pain undid
her simple dreams
she sipped the cold bitter brew
of life
and shivering in her agony
she longed for death.

Ode to Mary

(written by Mary's sister, Helen G. Ashley)

I saw a poem walk by
Her name is Mary
Structured like a sonnet
As structured as a castle,
She writes.
She makes poems as she watches furrows of
Marl fold under a plow
She ferrets out lines of poetry as the wind
Sieves through her hair.
Mary is a poem.
She is the embodiment of artistry
As she ambulates across a lea.
On the lea, she gathers verse.
"Poetry," she muses "Maybe it's a bird
A flamingo digging its long and fragile legs
In a frothy and steaming lake
Then glides away
"A slide where children play
A woman sweeping dust
A steel beam growing rust
A line collecting clothes

Puffs of clouds pushing planes
"And coffee pots
A quiet resting spot.
And Egypt?" she went on,
"There are anthologies of poetry in the pyramids
They are ripe for picking.
I will gather them and put them in a book."
I know Mary.
Once she turned a weathered
Locust shingle into a masterpiece with her inscription
Of metered verse.
She gathers wherever she goes.
I saw a poem walk by.
Her name is Mary.

Shadows

Striated lines of gold
  fell behind the trees
   black shadows took me
   into their hold—
    I was the saddest I'd ever been
    for sadness had my friend.

I walked in shadows
   as eerie silence had me mesmerized
   I had known happiness, then it died
   now I can say with no amends—
my Shadow is my sister
  my sister is my friend.

Dedication

Dear Helen,
Do you remember
How we sang as we drove the cows homeward
Me alto and you soprano
How we carried large buckets of water up the hill
from the spring
As we sang and quoted the poems we'd made
Until we discovered Keats, Shelly, Longfellow,
Kenley and Poe in our literature books
And quoted the ones we loved.
You skipped as you sang out, "Piping down the
valleys wild, Piping songs of merry glee.."
I chimed in "Out of the night That cover me Black
as the pit from pole to pole..
From Henley's poem "Invictus."
Then from Keats's "Ozymandias"
"...and the lone and level lands stretched far away."
Those were the days of our youth
Searching in poetry for beauty and truth.
Remember, Helen, Remember!